For the Teacher

This reproducible study guide consists of instructional material to use in conjunction with the novel *Night*. Written in chapter-by-chapter format, the guide contains a synopsis, pre-reading activities, vocabulary and comprehension exercises, as well as extension activities to be used as follow-up to the novel.

NOVEL-TIES are either for whole class instruction using a single title or for group instruction where each group uses a different novel appropriate to its reading level. Depending upon the amount of time allotted to it in the classroom, each novel, with its guide and accompanying lessons, may be completed in two to four weeks.

The first step in using NOVEL-TIES is to distribute to each student a copy of the novel and a folder containing all of the duplicated worksheets. Begin instruction by selecting several pre-reading activities in order to set the stage for the reading ahead. Vocabulary exercises for each chapter always precede the reading so that new words will be reinforced in the context of the book. Use the questions on the chapter worksheets for class discussion or as written exercises.

The benefits of using NOVEL-TIES are numerous. Students read good literature in the original, rather than in abridged or edited form. The good reading habits formed by practice in focusing on interpretive comprehension and literary techniques will be transferred to the books students read independently. Passive readers become active, avid readers.

Novel-Ties® are printed on recycled paper.

SYNOPSIS

This autobiographical novel is one survivor's emotionally searing account of life in Nazi concentration camps of World War II.

The small Romanian town of Sighet was the home of the Wiesel family who had four children—three daughters and a son, Eliezer. Eliezer, the narrator of this novel, was a devout student of the Talmud and the mystical teachings of the Kabbala.

Despite the warnings of Moshe the Beadle, who had witnessed Nazi atrocities, the Jews of Sighet believed that Germany was doomed and that they were too far from the fighting to be in danger. Then, in the spring of 1944, Germans descended on Sighet, rounded up the Jews, ordered them into ghettos, took away their valuables, and finally forced them into train cars built to hold cattle.

The train carried the Wiesels and their neighbors to Birkenau, a concentration camp which served as an entrance to Auschwitz. There the family was separated: the men were sent in one direction, the women in another. Frightened by this separation, the fourteen-year-old Eliezer desperately held on to his father's hand. The men were then examined by the infamous Dr. Mengele. The weak were put to death immediately; the strong and healthy—like Eliezer and his father—were spared. On their way to their barracks, the prisoners had to pass a ditch where bodies were being burned.

After three weeks in Auschwitz, the group to which Eliezer and his father belonged was forced to march to a nearby camp called Buna. There they had to cope with hunger, disease, beatings, the forcible removal of possessions such as shoes and gold fillings, tattooing, being forced to perform slave labor, and the dreaded "selections," during which the physically infirm were killed.

As the war dragged on and the Allies advanced, conditions in the camp became even worse. Food, always in short supply, became even more scarce. Allied bombings incited sabotage or resistance. These conditions led Eliezer to renounce God for having abandoned the Jews.

With the arrival of winter came the news that the Red Army was advancing. Buna was evacuated and the prisoners were forced to march through snow and ice for several days until they reached a train yard. Thousands of men died on this "Death March." Those who survived were crammed into open cattle cars and taken to Buchenwald, a concentration camp in the heart of Germany.

During the ten days they rode in the train, almost ninety percent of the men died. By the time they reached Buchenwald, Eliezer's father was deathly ill. Eliezer struggled with conflicting emotions—the desire to help his father and the desire to save his own life. On January 28, 1945, Eliezer climbed into the bunk above his father and went to sleep. When he awoke the next morning, his father was gone and another prisoner had taken his place.

With the death of Eliezer's father, the narrative nears an end. In a few terse concluding paragraphs, the narrator describes the last few days in the camp. He concludes by describing the haunted look in his eyes, as though a corpse was looking back at him from a mirror.

BACKGROUND INFORMATION: THE HOLOCAUST

The Holocaust refers to the systematic extermination of the Jewish people in Europe during the years that Adolf Hitler and the Nazis were in power in Germany (1933–1945). During that period, six million of Europe's nine million Jews were murdered, most of them in the infamous gas chambers and crematoria of the death camps.

Hitler, who had a pathological hatred of Jews, came to power in 1933 during a time of high unemployment and economic chaos. Using the Jews as scapegoats for Germany's problems, he roused the people with a virulently anti-Semitic program and a plan to build a pure and superior German "master race."

Hitler's craving for power and domination led to his invasion of European countries beginning in 1939. As world war ensued, Hitler put into action his plan for the "Final Solution"—the extermination of all Jews. The first death camp began operating at the village of Chelmo in December 1941, and soon other camps were built. Some camps existed only for killing entire trainloads of people. Others, such as Auschwitz-Birkenau and Buna, were death and labor camps where a small percentage of people were kept alive as slave labor. At Auschwitz, two thousand people at a time could be killed in the large gas chambers, and almost five thousand bodies could be burned in ovens in a single day. Valuables were taken from the prisoners, and gold was smelted down. Camp barbers shaved prisoners' hair, which was then sold to German companies for use in coat linings and as mattress stuffing.

It was not until Germany's defeat in 1945 that the world became fully aware of the incredible atrocities of the Holocaust. To this day, it is difficult to comprehend the enormity of this terrible human tragedy.

AUTHOR INFORMATION

Elie Wiesel was born in the Transylvanian town of Sighet, Romania, on September 30, 1928, the third of four children born to Shlomo and Sarah Wiesel. He was eleven years old at the beginning of World War II, and only fourteen when the Jews of Sighet were deported to the Nazi concentration camp at Auschwitz-Birkenau.

After the war, Wiesel settled in France where he studied at the Sorbonne and worked as a translator and eventually as a reporter. It was as a reporter that he met the famous French novelist and Nobel Prize winner François Mauriac. Mauriac urged Wiesel to break his vow of silence and tell the world about his experiences in the concentration camps. The story of those experiences was written in Yiddish and first published in 1956 as an eight-hundred page book entitled *Un di Velt Hot Geshvign* (*And the World Has Remained Silent*). The book was shortened to one hundred pages and translated into French (*La Nuit*) in 1958 and into English (*Night*) in 1960. Wiesel's wife Marion did a new translation of the book, which was published in 2006.

Wiesel moved to the United States in 1956 and became a citizen in 1963. In 1980 he was appointed chairman of the United States Holocaust Memorial Council. He has been the recipient of many awards, among them the 1985 Congressional Medal of Achievement and the 1986 Nobel Peace Prize, which he received for his message of "peace and atonement and human dignity."

GLOSSARY

achtung	attention
Appelplatz	place for roll call (*Appel*) in a concentration camp
Aryan	according to Nazi belief, a white Gentile (non-Jew)
Blockälteste	barrack chief in a concentration camp
Fascist	of or relating to dictatorial control by means of militant nationalism, terror, censorship, and racism
Gestapo	Nazi internal security police, from *geheim* (secret) + *staat* (state) + *polizei* (police)
ghetto	section of a city where Jews were required to live
Hasidic	of or relating to a Jewish reform movement founded in eastern and central Europe in the 1700s by Israel ben Eliezer, known as *Baal Shem Tov* (1700–1760)
Kabbala	mystical teachings that attempt to unravel the hidden meaning of Hebrew scriptures
Kaddish	Jewish prayer recited after the death of a close relative
Kapo	foreman of the individual huts in a concentration camp
Kommandant	commanding officer of a concentration camp
Lagerälteste	concentration camp chief
Moses Maimonides	(1135–1204) greatest Jewish scholar of the Middle Ages
Dr. Josef Mengele	(1911–1979?) Nazi doctor who conducted medical experiments on inmates of Auschwitz, escaped to South America at the end of World War II
mysticism	experience of the immediacy of God
Passover	holiday commemorating the biblical exodus of the Jews from Egypt
phylacteries	two small leather boxes containing Hebrew scriptures that are strapped to the forehead and arm during weekday morning worship
Rosh Hashanah	Jewish New Year, usually occurs in September
Shavuot	Jewish holiday celebrating the harvest season
SS	special security force of the Nazi party, from *Schultz* (defense) + *Staffel* (echelon)
Talmud	religious authority of Orthodox Judaism consisting of a collection of ancient rabbinical writings
the Temple	building in ancient Jerusalem that was the center of Jewish worship
Yom Kippur	also called Day of Atonement, a holy day ten days after Rosh Hashanah, celebrated by fasting and prayer

PRE-READING QUESTIONS AND ACTIVITIES

1. Elie Wiesel, author of *Night*, was the 1986 recipient of the Nobel Peace Prize. Do some research to learn the history of this prestigious award. Who are some of the recipients of the Nobel Peace Prize? What are their backgrounds? What kind of novel do you think a winner of the peace prize might have written, and why?

2. Read the Author Information on page two of this study guide. *Night* is called an autobiographical novel. How can a novel be autobiographical? What do you expect an autobiographical novel to contain? How might it differ from pure fiction or autobiography?

3. **Cooperative Learning Activity:** Read the Background Information on page two of this study guide and do some additional research to find out more about the Holocaust. Then brainstorm with a small group of classmates to fill in the first two columns of a K-W-L chart, such as the one below. When you finish the book, return to the chart and complete the third column.

The Holocaust

What I Know −K−	What I Want to Learn −W−	What I Learned −L−

4. **Social Studies Connection:** Individually, or in a cooperative learning group, review what you know about World War II in Europe. Then do some research as necessary to create a time-line of the major events in that war.

5. **Geography Connection:** Find a map showing Europe in 1944 in a social studies textbook, on the Internet, or in the library. Locate as many of these places as possible: Transylvania, Birkenau, Auschwitz, Buna, Gleiwitz, and Buchenwald. Use the scale to calculate the distances between these locations.

6. Have you read any other books about the Holocaust set in Europe during World War II? If so, when and where were these stories set? What did you learn about life at that time?

7. Read the preface to the new translation at the beginning of *Night*. What insights does it give you into this version of the book? In your own words, explain why it was important to Elie Wiesel to publish this new translation.

8. Wiesel has used the framing devices of an initiation and a journey to structure this novel. Think about other books you have read that have been organized this way. What was the outcome of the experience for the main character? The main character of *Night* is a teenage boy. Why are initiation and journey narratives typically about teenagers?

Pre-Reading Questions and Activities (cont.)

9. *Night* deals with the subject of religious prejudice. Are there any groups in your community who are objects of prejudice? What is being done to address this problem and assure fair treatment for everyone?

10. A critic said that Wiesel has:

    > unwittingly assumed the role of prophet, cautioning against
    > another Auschwitz, linking the burning ovens to the burning
    > Hiroshima, recognizing the infectiousness of evil and destruction,
    > and the callousness of the witnesses, the comfortably uninvolved.*

    How do you think Wiesel will try to keep the readers of his novel from being "comfortably uninvolved"?

*From *Contemporary Literary Criticism*, Volume 3, p. 527. (Detroit: Gale Research, 1975.)

PAGES 3 – 22 [Hill and Wang Edition]

Vocabulary: Use the context to determine the meaning of the underlined word in each of the following sentences. Then compare your definition with a dictionary definition.

1. Some Jews in Sighet <u>insinuated</u> that Moishe told his tales of terror to gain their pity.

   Your definition_____

   Dictionary definition _____

2. Eliezer advised his father to <u>liquidate</u> the family business and move to Palestine while there was still time.

   Your definition_____

   Dictionary definition _____

3. The Jews in Sighet found the news that German troops had penetrated Hungarian territory to be <u>disquieting</u>.

   Your definition_____

   Dictionary definition _____

4. Nazi officers were <u>billeted</u> in private homes in the towns they invaded.

   Your definition_____

   Dictionary definition _____

5. Eliezer's father, a good story teller, told <u>anecdotes</u> to ease people's fears and tensions.

   Your definition_____

   Dictionary definition _____

6. People clung to the hope that the order to evacuate Sighet would be <u>rescinded</u>.

   Your definition_____

   Dictionary definition _____

7. Since it was forbidden to break rank, some of the Jewish police <u>surreptitiously</u> obtained water for the parched deportees.

   Your definition_____

   Dictionary definition _____

Pages 3 – 22 (cont.)

Questions:

1. Why does Wiesel begin his novel with the account of Moshe the Beadle?

2. Why did the Jews of Sighet choose to believe the London radio reports rather than Moshe?

3. Why was it ironic that the leaders of the Jewish community were arrested during the celebration of Passover?

4. Why did Eliezer say that the ghetto was "ruled by delusion"?

5. Why did the Gestapo keep the destination of the deportees a secret from them?

6. Why did Eliezer begin to hate the Hungarian police?

7. What did the condition of the synagogue on the eve of deportation reveal to the Jews about their captors?

Questions for Discussion:

1. The Jews of Sighet didn't listen to Moshe the Beadle or to friendly servants, like Martha, who offered to hide and protect them. Could Moshe or Martha have done more to convince the Jews of their danger?

2. Do you think you and your family would be able to leave your country if an unfriendly government came into power? Where would you go? For whom would departure be more difficult—the young or the old?

Literary Devices:

I. *Simile*—A simile is a figure of speech in which a comparison between two unlike objects is stated directly using the words "like" or "as." For example:

> By eight o'clock in the morning, weariness had settled into our veins, our limbs, our brains, like molten lead.

What is being compared?

_____

How is the use of simile more effective than saying, "By eight o'clock we were very tired"?

_____

_____

Pages 3 – 22 (cont.)

II. *Metaphor*—A metaphor is a figure of speech in which a comparison between two unlike objects is suggested or implied. For example:

> The stars were but sparks of the immense conflagration that was consuming us. Were this conflagration to be extinguished one day, nothing would be left in the sky but extinct stars and unseeing eyes.

To what is the conflagration being compared?

_____

Why is this an apt comparison?

_____

_____

III. *Symbolism*—A symbol is an object, an event, or a character that represents an idea or a set of ideas.

What did the emblems on the German helmets symbolize?

_____

_____

What did the yellow star symbolize?

_____

_____

IV. *Point of View*—Point of view in literature refers to the person telling the story. There are three possible points of view in a novel:

- *First-person narrator* who, as a character, tells the story as he or she experienced it.
- *Third-person limited narrator* who knows what one character is doing and thinking
- *Third-person omniscient narrator* who knows what all the characters are doing and thinking

Which point of view has Wiesel chosen? What are the advantages and limitations of this point of view?

_____

_____

_____

_____

Pages 3 – 22 (cont.)

V. *Dramatic Irony*—Dramatic irony is a device used in fiction or drama, when characters are ignorant of something that the reader or members of the audience understand. In what way is the deportation of the Jews an example of dramatic irony?

_____

_____

_____

Writing Activity:

Imagine you are Eliezer's mother or father and write a letter to a relative in the United States describing recent events in your country.

SPECIAL ACTIVITY

Language Study: The Language of Prejudice

The Nazis tried to dehumanize the Jews by referring to them as animals. Wiesel used animal imagery to emphasize the plight of the Jews. Use this chart to record animal references as you read the novel. The first one has been done for you.

Page	Animal Imagery	Page	Animal Imagery
17	like beaten dogs		

When you have finished the novel, return to this chart and describe the cumulative effect of these animal images.

PAGES 23 – 28

Vocabulary: Draw a line from each word on the left to its definition on the right. Then use the numbered words to fill in the blanks in the sentences below.

1. intolerable   a. so as to be airtight
2. constraints   b. devoutly religious
3. irrevocably   c. restrictions
4. hermetically   d. foul smell
5. pious   e. bottomless depth
6. abyss   f. unbearable
7. stench   g. irreversibly; once and for all

. . . .

1. Once they left their community, young people ignored the social _____ that had regulated their lives in the past.

2. As a(n) _____ student of the Talmud and of the kabbala, Eliezer had always lived his life as an observant Jew.

3. When the doors of the train were nailed shut, the Jews felt as though they had been _____ sealed into the cattle cars.

4. With little ventilation and no sanitation, the air in the train became _____.

5. The _____ inside a closed train without sanitary facilities was overwhelming.

6. As they traveled by train to an unknown destination, the passengers felt as though a(n) _____ was opening beneath their feet.

7. Once inside the train, the Jews found the world they had known _____ lost to them.

Questions:

1. Why does Wiesel point out the countryside outside the train?

2. What might have been the source of Madame Schächter's visions of fire?

3. Many prophecies in the Bible begin with words such as "Hear ye this" or "Listen unto me." What similar sentence was used by both Moshe the Beadle and by Madame Schächter? Why does Wiesel put identical words into the mouths of these two characters?

4. What did the treatment of Madame Schächter reveal about what was happening to the community?

5. Why was it significant that no one on the train had ever heard of *Auschwitz*?

Pages 23 – 28 (cont.)

Questions for Discussion:

1. Why do you think the Jews of Sighet did not fear the worst and prepare themselves for the events of 1944?
2. Do you think rebellion could have been a choice for the community?
3. If you had been in the cattle car, how would you have reacted to Madam Schächter? What, if anything, would you have done differently from the other passengers?

Literary Element: Style

Style refers to the way language is used to express an author's individuality and the theme of the novel. A remarkable feature of this novel is Wiesel's control of language. He usually reports events without commenting on them, letting the events speak for themselves.

Find a paragraph in which horrific events are reported concisely, without emotion or commentary. How does this style of writing achieve Wiesel's purpose? What does it reveal about Wiesel himself?

Literary Device: Foreshadowing

Foreshadowing refers to the clues an author provides to suggest what will happen later in the novel. What do Madame Schächter's visions foreshadow?

_____

_____

Writing Activity:

Contrast—such as that between the blooming countryside and the interior of the train—is a technique that can be used to make a point indelible. Write a short essay in which you deliberately contrast external surroundings with inner emotions.

PAGES 29 – 46

Vocabulary: Synonyms are words with similar meanings. Draw a line from each word in column A to its synonym in column B. Then use the words in column A to fill in the blanks in the sentences below.

A	B
1. tumult	a. strewn
2. imperative	b. clarity
3. notorious	c. lectured
4. interspersed	d. shriveled
5. lucidity	e. commotion
6. harangued	f. infamous
7. wizened	g. crucial

. . . .

1. In moments of _____, the prisoners realized that there was no escape.

2. Dr. Josef Mengele's medical experiments on prisoners made him _____.

3. A small man with a(n) _____ face sought information about his family..

4. Eliezer felt it was _____ for him and his father to stay together.

5. The SS officer _____ the prisoners about life at Auschwitz.

6. There was _____ when the train first unloaded, with people scattered everywhere.

7. The prisoner's words were _____ with sobs after encountering a loved one.

Questions:
1. How did the SS man as he spoke to the new arrivals reveal his feelings toward the Jews?

2. Why was Eliezer so determined to remain with his father?

3. What does the narrator mean when he speaks of being "condemned to live"?

4. Why did Eliezer feel he had become a different person in just one night? What evidence is there that he was right?

Pages 29 – 46 (cont.)

5. What was the significance of the inscription "Work makes you free"?

6. Why were the prisoners tattooed?

7. Why did Stein no longer visit after he had been given the "real" news about his family?

8. Why did Eliezer and his father pretend that Mrs. Wiesel and Tzipora were in labor camps?

Questions for Discussion:

1. Why do you think Eliezer recited the Kaddish in spite of himself? Would you have prayed under similar circumstances?

2. Do you think that knowing Elie Wiesel survived the camps detracts from the horror he conveyed?

Social Studies Connections:

1. Do some research to learn about Dr. Josef Mengele. Learn about his role at Auschwitz and what happened to him after the war.

2. When Eliezer stated that the world would never tolerate the Nazis' crimes against the Jews, his father responded that the "world is not interested in us." Do some research to find out what other countries knew about the fate of the Jews during the Holocaust and what, if anything, they did about it. Then decide if you agree with Eliezer or his father.

Literary Devices:

I. *Metaphor*—Below, Wiesel states the central metaphor of his novel:

> Never shall I forget that night, the first night in camp, that turned my life into one long night seven times sealed.

What is being compared?

_____

What does this metaphor reveal about conditions at the camp and about the course of future action in the novel?

_____

_____

Pages 29 – 46 (cont.)

II. *Allusion*—An allusion is a reference to a famous historical, mythological, biblical, or literary person or event.

- One of the older prisoners said, "You mustn't give up hope, even now as the sword hangs over our heads." In Greek mythology, Damocles was a courtier in the court of Dionysius. After hearing Damocles endlessly praise his power and happiness, Dionysius decided to teach Damocles a lesson about the precarious nature of power. He forced Damocles to sit at a banquet with a sword suspended over his head by a single strand of hair. How does this allusion add to your understanding of the plight of the Jews?

_____

_____

_____

_____

- The Bible contains the story of Job, an upright man whose family, possessions, and health were destroyed as trials of his faith in God. Explain why Eliezer sympathized with Job.

_____

_____

Writing Activity:

Write a short story in which you use one of the two allusions above. For example, you might write about a Nazi war criminal who, after the war, lived with a sword hanging over his head.

PAGES 47 – 65

Vocabulary: Choose a word from the Word Box to replace the underlined word or phrase in each of the following sentences. Write the word you choose on the line below the sentence.

	WORD BOX	
altruistic	dissipated	sabotage
cynical	imprudent	untenable

1. The distinguished musician wore a <u>scornful</u> smile when he was informed that he could not play German music.

   _____

2. <u>Destruction by enemy agents</u> was suspected when the power station at the camp was blown up.

   _____

3. The German guard's affection for the children was not entirely <u>unselfish</u>.

   _____

4. It would have been <u>unwise</u> for any of the prisoners to complain to the guards.

   _____

5. It became <u>indefensible</u> to Eliezer to protect his gold crown by allowing his father to be beaten.

   _____

6. After the raid, the sounds of the American plane <u>vanished</u> as the aircraft retreated.

   _____

Questions:

1. Earlier in the novel, Eliezer said the flames burned away the child that he had been, leaving only a body. In this section of the novel, he said he was even less than a body. What had he become, and why?

2. Why does the author admit to being angry with his father when Idek beat him?

3. What sad lesson did Eliezer learn after attempting to hold on to his shoes and his gold crown?

4. Why did Idek have Eliezer beaten instead of having him killed?

Pages 47 – 65 (cont.)

5. How did the prisoners feel about the man who crawled to the soup cauldron during the air-raid?

6. Why weren't the prisoners afraid to die in a bomb blast?

7. Why did Eliezer describe his reactions to the hangings in terms of the flavor of the soup?

Questions for Discussion:

1. Why do you think the Nazis played music in the camps? Although clearly not their intention, do you think that the music helped the inmates in any way?

2. Eliezer, Yossi, and Tibi felt that their parents had "lacked the courage to sell everything and emigrate while there was still time." Do you agree that the boys' parents lacked courage?

Literary Devices

I. *Flash-forward*—A flash-forward occurs when a future event is interjected into the chronological sequence of events in a novel. This device is used to provide information that would otherwise not be available to the reader, and it is sometimes used to relieve tension. What is the flash-forward in this section of the novel?

_____

What information does it provide? How does it serve to relieve tension?

_____

_____

II. *Metaphor*—What is being compared in this metaphor?

> . . . we saw three gallows, three black ravens . . . .

_____

Why is this an apt comparison?

_____

_____

Writing Activity:

Since the publication of *Night*, theologians from all religions have attempted to answer the question posed in this section of the novel: *Where was God?* Write an essay in which you attempt to answer this question.

PAGES 66 – 84

Vocabulary: Antonyms are words with opposite meanings. Draw a line from each word in column A to its antonym in column B. Then use the words in column A to fill in the blanks in the sentences below.

A	B
1. agitated	a. fullness
2. submission	b. deterrent
3. lament	c. resistance
4. void	d. uncertain
5. emaciated	e. calm
6. decisive	f. fat
7. incentive	g. celebrate

. . . .

1. After Eliezer rebelled against God, he felt a great _____ in his heart.

2. Most inmates felt so beaten that they lost the _____ to fight to survive.

3. With a(n) _____ gesture, Dr. Mengele wrote down the numbers of the men who were not in top physical condition.

4. The guards starved and beat the inmates into _____.

5. One shriveled-up man, more _____ than the rest, asked why his name had been written down.

6. Everyone at the camp was _____ as tension filled the air on the last day of the Jewish year.

7. Feeling numb, the inmates were no longer able to _____ the death of fellow prisoners.

Questions:

1. Why were the prisoners tense on the last day of the Jewish year?
2. Why did Eliezer say, "It was Yom Kippur year-round"?
3. How did the head of Eliezer's block treat the men under his command? Why did he treat them this way?
4. The head of the block told the men to run "as if the devil were after you." What is ironic about this advice?
5. What does Wiesel mean when he speaks of "the crucible of death"?
6. Was Akiba Drumer a victim of the selection, or of something else?
7. Why did Eliezer leave the infirmary rather than wait in camp for liberation with the rest of the sick?

Pages 66 – 84 (cont.)

Questions for Discussion:

1. Do you think any of the prisoners had a sense of hope for a better future?

2. Do you think a person in a concentration camp could continue to believe in God? Might such a value system affect a person's ability to survive?

3. Do you think Eliezer made the right choice in leaving the infirmary? Do you think he still would have left had he known that staying meant liberation?

Literary Devices:

I. *Symbolism*—What did the knife and spoon symbolize to Eliezer?

_____

_____

II. *Irony*—Irony, as opposed to dramatic irony, is a figure of speech in which the intent is expressed in words that have the opposite meaning from what is expected. Explain the irony in this passage:

> I have more faith in Hitler than in anyone else. He alone has kept his promises, all his promises, to the Jewish people.

_____

_____

III. *Repetition*—Repetition is the repeated use of any element of language, such as a word, phrase, sound, or rhythmic pattern, in close proximity. For example:

> The last night in Buna. Once more, the last night. The last night at home, the last night in the ghetto, the last night in the cattle car, and, now, the last night in Buna. How much longer would our lives be lived from one "last night" to the next?

What effect does Wiesel achieve with this use of repetition?

_____

_____

Writing Activity:

Write about a time when you or someone you know suffered from a misuse of power. Discuss the motivations of those in power and the effect of their behavior on its victim.

PAGES 85 – 103

Vocabulary: Word analogies are equations in which the first pair of words has the same relationship as the second pair of words. For example: EMBARKATION is to ARRIVAL as BEGINNING is to ENDING. Both pairs of words are opposites. Choose the best word from the Word Box to complete each of the analogies below.

WORD BOX		
apathy	excruciating	plaintive
disheveled	grimace	poignant

1. SOOTHING is to COMFORTING as AGONIZING is to _____.

2. HIDEOUS is to BEAUTIFUL as _____ is to NEAT.

3. MOURNFUL is to _____ as GRACEFUL is to ELEGANT.

4. _____ is to FACE as CONTORTION is to BODY.

5. VIGOROUS is to FEEBLE as UNEMOTIONAL is to _____.

6. CONFUSION is to CLARITY as _____ is to INTEREST.

Questions:

1. Why did the Nazis make the prisoners run?

2. Why was the shed preferable to the silence of the outside?

3. Why was Eliezer glad that he had forgotten seeing Rabbi Eliahu's son?

4. How was it possible for Juliek to have retained his violin in the camp?

5. Why was Eliezer touched by the "eerily poignant little corpse" of the violin, when hundreds of human corpses left him unmoved?

4. What was the significance of the prisoners' animal-like attack on the scraps of bread?

5. What points is Wiesel making in the story about the woman who threw coins to young divers?

Pages 85 – 103 (cont.)

Questions for Discussion:

1. When Eliezer feared that his foot was frozen, he said, "The important thing was not to dwell on it. Especially now. Leave those thoughts for later." Was this good advice?

2. Why do you think that Eliezer's father smiled after his son woke him up? Why is it something that Eliezer will never forget?

3. Do you agree with Eliezer's statement toward the end of the train ride that "All boundaries had been crossed"?

Literary Devices:

I. *Personification*—Personification is a literary device in which an author grants lifelike qualities to non-human objects, animals, or ideas. For example:

> Death, which was settling in all around me, silently, gently. It would seize upon a sleeping person, steal into him and devour him bit by bit.

What is being personified?

_____

How does this use of personification maximize the prisoners' plight?

_____

_____

II. *Metaphor*—What is being compared in the following metaphor?

> And so he [Rabbi Eliahu] left, as he had come: a shadow swept away by the wind.

_____

How does this comparison help you to visualize the scene?

_____

III. *Symbolism*—What does the broken violin symbolize?

_____

_____

Writing Activity:

In these two sections of the novel, we meet or learn about three pairs of fathers and sons—Eliezer and his father, Rabbi Eliahu and his son, and the man who tried to hide the piece of bread and his son Meir. Write an essay in which you compare and contrast the relationships between these fathers and sons.

PAGES 104 – 115

Vocabulary: Use the context to determine the meaning of the underlined word in each of the following sentences. Then circle the letter of the word you choose.

1. The guards beat the prisoners to control them but to no avail; chaos ensued.

   a. benefit   b. harm   c. loss   d. intention

2. Eliezer's father had become feeble and vulnerable, no longer able to deal with the horrors of the camp.

   a. stubborn   b. eager   c. sullen   d. helpless

3. Suffering from a serious illness, the prisoner was prostrate on his cot.

   a. prone   b. comfortable   c. upright   d. delirious

4. When they first arrived at Buchenwald, Eliezer stayed riveted to his father for fear of losing him.

   a. loyal   b. accessible   c. bound   d. near

5. For the SS to be late for a prisoner count was unprecedented at the camp.

   a. common   b. unusual   c. frightening   d. encouraging

6. When Eliezer looked in the mirror, he saw a corpse contemplating him.

   a. imitating   b. observing   c. teasing   d. consoling

Questions:

1. Why did arguing with his father seem like arguing with Death itself to Eliezer?

2. What did the air-raid sirens reveal about the status of the war?

3. What role reversal took place during the final illness of Eliezer's father?

4. What did Eliezer's wish to "set the whole world on fire" reveal?

5. Why did Eliezer have conflicted feelings about his father's illness?

6. Why did the resistance movement wait so long to act?

7. Why did none of the prisoners think about revenge after they were liberated?

Pages 104 – 115 (cont.)

Questions for Discussion:

1. Do you agree with Eliezer that he was just like Rabbi Eliahu's son? In what ways were they alike? In what ways were they different?

2. Eliezer was convinced that, near death, his father saw the truth in all things. What truths do you think his father saw?

3. What might have happened to Eliezer and his father if the bond between them had not been as strong as it was?

4. What physical and emotional problems do you think survivors of the concentration camp faced?

5. What physical and emotional qualities do you think Eliezer Wiesel possessed to make him a survivor? Do you think luck or fate played a role?

Literary Element: Conflict

Conflict in literature refers to the clash of opposing forces. There are three major forms of conflict. Use the chart below to record each form of conflict in the novel.

Person *vs.* Person	
Person *vs.* Nature	
Person *vs.* Self	

Social Studies Connection:

Wiesel was in Buchenwald from January to April of 1945. Do some research to learn what was happening in Germany during the last months of the war. How does your understanding of the larger picture help you understand the lives of the prisoners in the concentration camps?

Writing Activity:

Write an essay in which you consider whether or not the image contained in the last two sentences is a fitting ending to this story. Support your opinion with reasons and examples.

CLOZE ACTIVITY

The following excerpt is taken from pages 94 – 95 of *Night*. Read it through completely and then go back and fill in the blank spaces with words that makes sense. When you have finished, you may compare your language with that of the author.

Those were my thoughts when I heard the sound of a violin. A violin in a dark barrack where the _____[1] were piled on top of the living? _____[2] was this madman who played the violin _____,[3] at the edge of his own grave? _____[4] was it a hallucination?

It had to _____[5] Juliek.

He was playing a fragment of _____[6] Beethoven concerto. Never before had I heard _____[7] a beautiful sound. In such silence.

How _____[8] he succeeded in disengaging himself? To slip _____[9] from under my body without my feeling _____?[10]

The darkness enveloped us. All I could _____[11] was the violin, and it was as _____[12] Juliek's soul had become his bow. He _____[13] playing his life. His whole being was _____[14] over the strings. His unfulfilled hopes. His _____[15] past, his extinguished future. He played that _____[16] he would never play again.

I shall _____[17] forget Juliek. How could I forget this _____[18] given before an audience of the dead _____[19] dying?

Even today, when I hear that _____[20] piece by Beethoven, my eyes close and _____[21] of the darkness emerges the pale and _____[22] face of my Polish comrade bidding farewell _____[23] an audience of dying men.

I don't _____[24] how long he played. I was overcome _____[25] sleep. When I awoke at daybreak, I _____[26] Juliek facing me, hunched over, dead. Next to him lay his violin, trampled, an eerily poignant little corpse.

POST-READING ACTIVITIES AND DISCUSSION QUESTIONS

1. Return to the K-W-L chart that you began in the Pre-Reading Questions and Activities on page four of this study guide. Based on the knowledge you have gained, correct any errors and add new information to column three. Then compare your responses with those of your classmates.

2. Return to the chart you began on page eight. Describe the cumulative effect of the animal images.

3. How are Elie Wiesel, the author, and Eliezer Wiesel, the narrator, the same? How are they different? Consider the significance of the first name used by Wiesel for himself as author and for himself as character.

4. The chronological plot structure of *Night* can be represented in this way:

   What structure is made evident in this diagram? How do the sections of the novel balance each other?

5. *Night* deals with change—physical, emotional, religious. Use a chart such as the one below to record the changes in Eliezer during the course of the novel.

	Eliezer at the Beginning of the Novel	**Eliezer at the End of the Novel**
Physical		
Emotional		
Religious		

6. The theme of a novel is its central idea or the author's message. Some of the themes in *Night* are:
   - effect of prejudice on the human spirit
   - horror of war
   - basic nature of humanity as good or evil
   - relationship of God to humankind
   - fragility of existence
   - bond between parent and child

   Discuss how one of these themes, or any other important theme, is developed in the novel.

Post-Reading Activities and Discussion Questions (cont.)

7. Why do you think Elie Wiesel waited eleven years before writing about his experience in a Nazi concentration camp?

8. Having called his work an autobiographical novel, do you think Wiesel should have recorded events exactly as they occurred or was he justified in taking some artistic license?

9. **Cooperative Learning Activity:** No one can read *Night* without wondering how one's own behavior would have compared to that of Eliezer as a victim or to that of a German citizen who lived free of the camps during World War II. Discuss these issues with a small group of your classmates. Also discuss your reactions to this novel and evaluate its impact on your life.

10. Read Wiesel's Nobel Peace Prize acceptance speech on pages 117–120 of the book. With the following words, Wiesel vows to speak out against human suffering and humiliation:

    > We must take sides. Neutrality helps the oppressor, never the
    > victim. Silence encourages the tormentor, never the tormented.

    Has reading this book convinced you to adopt Wiesel's point of view? Which of his arguments do you find the most compelling, and why?

11. Despite the lessons of the Holocaust, anti-Semitism and instances of genocide continue to this day. Find evidence of this in the national and international pages of your newspaper. Contact the nearest chapter of the Anti-Defamation League of B'nai B'rith to learn about recent incidents of anti-Semitism.

12. Do some research to learn about the war crimes tribunal held at Nuremberg after World War II and prepare a report of your findings.

SUGGESTIONS FOR FURTHER READING

Appleman-Jurman, Alicia. *Alicia: My Story*. Random House.

Bishop, Claire H. *Twenty and Ten*. Penguin.

Bitton-Jackson, Livia. *I Have Lived a Thousand Years: Growing Up in the Holocaust*. Simon & Schuster.

* Boyne, John. *The Boy in the Striped Pajamas*. Random House.

Denes, Magda. *Castles Burning: A Child's Life in War*. W.W. Norton.

* Frank, Anne. *Anne Frank: The Diary of a Young Girl*. Random House.

* Greene, Bette. *Summer of My German Soldier*. Random House.

* Kerr, M.E. *Gentlehands*. HarperCollins.

Kuper, Jack. *Child of the Holocaust*. Penguin.

* Levitin, Sonia. *Journey to America*. Simon & Schuster.

* Lowry, Lois. *Number the Stars*. Random House.

Mazur, Harry. *The Last Mission*. Random House.

* Rhue, Morton. *The Wave*. Random House.

Richter, Hans P. *Friedrich*. Penguin.

_____. *I Was There*. Penguin.

Roth-Hano, Renee. *Touch Wood*. Penguin.

Sachs, Marilyn. *A Pocket Full of Seeds*. Penguin.

Sender, Ruth M. *The Cage*. Simon & Schuster.

_____. *To Life*. Penguin.

Serraillier, Ian. *Escape From Warsaw*. Scholastic.

Siegal, Aranka. *Upon the Head of the Goat*. Penguin.

ten Boom, Corrie. *The Hiding Place*. Random House.

* Yolen, Jane. *The Devil's Arithmetic*. Penguin.

* Zusak, Markus. *The Book Thief*. Random House.

Some Other Books by Elie Wiesel

The Accident. Farrar, Straus & Giroux.

All Rivers Run to the Sea: Memoirs. Random House.

A Beggar in Jerusalem. Random House.

Dawn. Random House.

Day. Hill and Wang.

The Gates of the Forest. Random House.

The Oath. Random House.

The Town Beyond the Wall. Schocken.

* NOVEL-TIES Study Guides are available for these titles.

ANSWER KEY

Pages 3 – 22

Vocabulary: 1. insinuated–suggested in an unpleasant way   2. liquidate–end a business by converting assets to cash   3. disquieting–disturbing   4. billeted–lodged in nonmilitary buildings   5. anecdotes–short humorous or interesting stories   6. rescinded–cancelled   7. surreptitiously–stealthy

Questions: 1. In many ways, Moshe's situation paralleled that of Wiesel. Moshe, who had been "saved miraculously," went back to tell the story of his "death." Wiesel, who had also been saved, used this novel to tell the story of his own spiritual death. 2. The news from London conveyed the impression that Germany would soon be defeated. The Jews of Sighet preferred to believe these comforting radio reports rather than the horrors described by Moshe. (Some readers may comment that news from London probably contained a good deal of propaganda intended to dishearten Germany and its allies and, thus, was not a totally reliable source of information.) 3. Since Passover celebrates the liberation of the Jews from captivity in Egypt, it is ironic that the homes of Jews were targeted in Sighet during Passover in 1944. 4. The ghetto was "ruled by delusion" since it was the inmates' own false optimism in the face of harsh reality that prevented them from rebelling in any way. 5. The Gestapo kept the destination of the deportees a secret so that they were easy to control; if they had known the truth, they might have rebelled. 6. Eliezer began to hate the Hungarian police because they treated his family with contempt and became their first oppressors. 7. The desecration of their house of worship impressed upon the Jews the utter contempt in which they were held by their captors.

Pages 23 – 28

Vocabulary: 1. f   2. c   3. g   4. a   5. b   6. e; 1. constraints   2. pious   3. hermetically   4. intolerable   5. stench   6. abyss   7. irrevocably

Questions: 1. The mention of the blossoming countryside provides a stark contrast to conditions inside the train. 2. We do not know for certain, but it is reasonable to assume that, in addition to hearing Moshe's stories, Madame Schächter had heard rumors about what was happening to Jews from other communities. 3. Both Moshe and Madame Schächter said, "Jews, listen to me." Wiesel uses this technique to indicate that both of these characters serve as prophets. 4. As they turned on each other, it revealed that the community was beginning to come undone. 5. The unfamiliarity of the name revealed how successful the Germans had been in keeping the death camps secret.

Pages 29 – 46

Vocabulary: 1. e   2. g   3. f   4. a   5. b   6. c; 1. lucidity   2. notorious   3. wizened   4. imperative   5. harangued   6. tumult   7. interspersed

Questions: 1. The callous indifference of the SS man underlined his contempt for the Jews. 2. Eliezer was determined to remain with his father because he was young, terrified of being alone, and had a strong bond with his father. 3. We usually speak of being condemned to die, but in a world where everything held dear was being exterminated, to go on living with that memory might seem to be a punishment. 4. Eliezer felt as if his soul had been invaded and eaten by a black flame. The evidence is that he already began to doubt his religion and failed to respond when his father was attacked. 5. The darker interpretation of this inscription was that prisoners would be free to live only as long as they were able to work. 6. In addition to being a record-keeping system, the tattoos were another way to further dehumanize the prisoners. Having taken away their homes, possessions, and security, the Nazis now wanted to take away their names, their very identities. 7. Stein undoubtedly learned that his wife and children were dead. Since they were his only reason for living, it must be assumed that soon after learning of their fate, he fell victim to the camp. 8. Eliezer and his father had seen Mrs. Wiesel and Tzipora directed to the line headed for the crematoria, so they were fairly certain the two were dead. However, they pretended otherwise not to kill any hope that the other might still have held.

Pages 47 – 65

Vocabulary: 1. cynical   2. sabotage 3. altruistic   4. imprudent   5. untenable   6. dissipated

Questions: 1. By the time he arrived in Buna, Eliezer saw himself as only a famished stomach; hunger dominated and controlled his life. 2. Although he felt it was a shameful admission, the author wants his readers to understand what life in the camps was capable of doing to a person. 3. Eliezer learned that it was pointless to try to retain personal possessions. If he had been willing to part with his shoes and gold crown immediately, he might have been able to barter for food or privileges. By trying to hold on to them, he lost them and any bargaining position he might have had. 4. Idek obviously decided that having Eliezer beaten in front of the other prisoners as an example was more effective than having him killed. 5. The prisoners had mixed emotions

about the man who crawled to the soup cauldron. Eliezer said they envied him, but never thought of admiring him. However, one sentence—"He was the one who dared."—casts doubt on that assertion. As victims, some of the prisoners probably *did* admire the man, even though they knew he was doomed. 6. When Eliezer said, "But we no longer feared death; at any event not this particular death," he meant that a quick death in a bomb blast held no horror for the prisoners, especially if the bomb destroyed the concentration camp as well. 7. Since Eliezer felt that he had become a famished stomach, it is natural that he would record his reactions to the hangings in terms of food.

Pages 66 – 84

Vocabulary: 1. e 2. c 3. g 4. a 5. f 6. d 7. b; 1. void 2. incentive 3. decisive 4. submission 5. emaciated 6. agitated 7. lament

Questions: 1. The prisoners were tense because they realized that the last day of the year could very well be their last day on earth. Some students might suggest that they were also uneasy about their religious beliefs because of the hardships they had endured. 2. Yom Kippur is a holy day marked by fasting and by prayers for the atonement of sins. Eliezer's bitter comment refers to the fact that the Jews had been starved (fasting) since their capture. In addition, those who had not lost their faith said prayers all the time. 3. The head of Eliezer's block was a German Jew who had been incarcerated for eleven years (since 1933). As a Jew, he tried to treat the men under his command with compassion. Before a selection, he gave them tips about how to pass the inspection. Sometimes his compassion compelled him to lie, and then he would shout at the men or shut himself away from them. 4. The irony in this advice is that the devil, in human form, really *was* after them 5. A crucible is a severe test or trial. Wiesel's reference to a "crucible of death" suggests that facing death is a severe trial for any human being. As a boy in a concentration camp, Eliezer ran from those who were selected to die. 6. Akiba Drumer died *in* the selection, but not *because* of it; he died because he had lost his faith. Once Akiba felt that God was no longer with him, he had no incentive to live. 7. Eliezer left the infirmary because he did not want to be separated from his father, with whom he had endured so much hardship and suffering.

Pages 85 – 103

Vocabulary: 1. excruciating 2. disheveled 3. plaintive 4. grimace 5. poignant 6. apathy

Questions: 1. The Nazis made the prisoners run because they wanted to be far away when the Russian army arrived. Also, the Nazis probably wanted to kill off more of the prisoners during the forced march. 2. The outside was like a cemetery, with the dead and dying not making a sound. 3. Eliezer saw that the rabbi's son had left him as he would a burden. He was glad that he did not have to relate this to the rabbi, and he did not want to consider that he might be capable of doing the same thing. 4. At Buna, Juliek had been assigned to the orchestra block. Prisoners who played in the orchestra must have been allowed to keep their musical instruments. 5. Hardened by the camps, by loss, by death, by starvation, and by inhumane treatment, Eliezer was still able to be moved by the purity and beauty of Juliek's music. 6. The prisoners' attack on the bread showed that the Nazis had succeeded in one respect: their prisoners had been reduced to animals. 7. Wiesel makes several points: that people do not always understand or think about the consequences of their actions; that cruelty is not limited to any one group of people; that a few of the Germans may have mistakenly thought that they were helping the prisoners by throwing bread to them.

Pages 104 – 115

Vocabulary: 1. a 2. d 3. a 4. c 5. b 6. b

Questions: 1. Eliezer's father, in a weakened condition, chose death over a life of suffering. 2. The increasing frequency of the air-raid alerts indicated that the Allies were moving ever closer to the center of Germany and that the war was, therefore, nearing its end. 3. Eliezer became the father figure as his father became more childlike. 4. Although Eliezer saw himself as only a famished stomach, his anger at the treatment of his father revealed that he was still a loving son. 5. Eliezer loved his father and wanted to help him, yet at the same time he knew his own chances of survival were compromised by caring for his father. 6. The most likely reasons that the resistance movement waited so long to act are that the men were weak and did not have enough weapons to take on the SS under normal conditions, but with the advance of the Russians and the resulting chaos, the odds were in their favor. 7. The prisoners had been deprived of so much for so long that their only thoughts were of survival. And after they had food and clothes, they were probably too weak to even contemplate revenge at the time.